Craven Langstroth Betts, H. Arthur Kennedy

The Perfume-Holder

A Persian love poem. Vol. 1

Craven Langstroth Betts, H. Arthur Kennedy

The Perfume-Holder
A Persian love poem. Vol. 1

ISBN/EAN: 9783337289508

Printed in Europe, USA, Canada, Australia, Japan

Cover: Foto ©Thomas Meinert / pixelio.de

More available books at **www.hansebooks.com**

THE PERFUME-HOLDER

A PERSIAN LOVE POEM
BY CRAVEN LANGSTROTH
BETTS

SAALFIELD & FITCH,
PUBLISHERS,
12 BIBLE HOUSE, ASTOR PLACE,
NEW YORK.

TO
R. G. W.

THE PERFUME-HOLDER.

FAIR Naishápúr, two hundred years ago,
   Then free and prosperous from the Turkish foe,
Like a bright jewel out of Allah's hand
Lay gleaming in the green Khorassan land.
Far to the east, the insidious desert soil
Strangled the verdure with its sandy coil,
But north and south, the languorous noon-day breeze
Waved the light leaves of lime and cypress trees
Across the hills, within whose broken row
The city glimmered in the vale below.
Along the road that led from Ispahan
Was heard the tinkling of the caravan,
Trailing its dusty, sinuous passage down
Unto the market of the wealthy town.

Piercing the hot and dazzling ether through
A hundred minarets burned against the blue.
The purple roofs of mosques, to Summer's smiles,
Flashed all their panoply of porcelain tiles,
While from their walls the names of Allah shone,
In many a bold and quaint device of stone.
Color and light cast everywhere their glow
Among the booths and houses, row on row;
It flamed from off the palace court-yard flags,
And blazoned even the cringing beggar's rags.
The ponds and fountains glittering steely-cold
The sun's keen alchemy changed to liquid gold,
And marble cupolas and awnings white
Flashed in full splendour of reflected light,
While green pomegranate leaf and pregnant vine
Caught deeper lustre from the ethereal shine.
Teeming with fierce and palpitating heat,
The sunbeams wove their network o'er the street,
And gleamed along the cream-white painted walls
Of gardens and the roofs of market stalls,
And showered a mist of yellow radiance down
O'er hill and valley, desert, wood, and town.

TWAS noon in Naishápúr—the gay bazaars
    Heaped with their wares from 'neath ten thousand
        stars
One ant-like, vast, conglomerate market made,
Cross-scored with throbbing avenues of trade.
But yet the hum of traffic even there
Hushed at the high Muezzin's call to prayer,
And too oppressive was the stare of day
For active toil along the market way.
Some moments longer surged the stir and bruit
Around the coffee stalls and booths of fruit,
A moment longer did the merchant stop
To close the little shutters of his shop,
Then in his slippers homeward hurried fast
To mid-day prayer and the noon's brief repast.
In the brass-workers' noisy bright bazaar
Stilled was the chaffering and the hammers' jar,
And silence, with its solemn, reverent grace,
Softly down spreading from reposeful space,
Rested an hour upon the market-place.

ONE man, a poor artificer of brass,
    Stirs not as forth the hurrying vendors pass;

But soon as stillness rests upon the street,
Springs from his cross-legged posture to his feet,
Puts by the lantern he had shaped that day,
Looks up and down the cleared, deserted way,
Takes down the bowl of curds and loaf of bread
That stand upon a shelf above his head,
Hooks up a curtain o'er the narrow space
Which forms his doorway to the market-place,
Casts one more look along the farther wall,
Then hides himself behind the portal shawl.

ONE might have heard within that curtain soon
        A tapping through the hot and quiet noon;
A strange man this—'tis sure for greed of gain
He doth at work the noontide hour remain;
It was his custom — no one notice took;
He was to all a strange and sealèd book;
No one came near him but to buy or sell;
They named him Selim the Unsociable.
That any one should think it worth his care
Why the brass-worker spent his hour of prayer
Behind his curtain, save for closer shade,
Had never on his fellows' minds been laid.

It well might seem that for such watchful heed
Was little use; — for there was naught, indeed,
Save vagrant dogs along the shining track,
Sleeping like pious Moslems, in a pack,
Snarling in dream, because the heated bricks
Smote them in poignant fancy like the kicks
Of Allah's Faithful—snapped their jaws in pain,
Then rolling over stretched their limbs again.

BUT there came one who in that quiet street
    Listened intently to the hammer's beat;
You might have marked him by his furtive eye
A man of cunning, dangerous, shrewd, and sly;
At Selim's booth he made a sudden stand,
Lifted the curtain with a stealthy hand
And peered within—a single ray of light
Flashed up a marvellous work upon his sight;
For, rested Selim's bended knees between,
Glowing with new and richest coppery sheen,
Engrossed with scrolls of purest arabesque,
A perfume-holder, airily grotesque,
Wrought all of brass, pierced round with lace designs
And burnished fine between the mottoed lines;

A miracle of rare and patient art
Informed by genius working from the heart,
Such as might hold the incense at the shrine
Of Allah or of Mahomet the Divine:—
One might forego all sense except the eyes
To be possessed of such a wondrous prize.

YOU in the misty amethystine West
    Know not with what a rare and pungent zest
The Persian in his drier purer air
Values his perfume even as his prayer.
The perfume-holder—an effeminate whim
To you—holds yet an honored place with him:
Scatter within it but some glowing coals,
Lo! from the brazier forth the perfume rolls,
Like the warm incense of the votive breath
From lovers' lips as they unclose in death!

TO lie awake in one bliss-haunted dream
    Where leaves are rustling and where fountains gleam,
Within a cool and lustrous colonnade,
While near, some large-eyed, love-enchanted maid
Leans, lily crowned, against a marble jar,

Caressing languidly her light guitar,
Her fingers glancing o'er the shimmering strings
Like play of moonbeams on soft bubbling springs,
Wooing the soul of melody divine
From murmuring streams and groves of haunted pine,
Her bosom heaving to the waves of sound
That have in one delicious languor drowned
The outer sense, leaving the spirit free
To revel in a swoon-like ecstasy—
And then to watch the perfume vapor curl
With many a slender and fantastic swirl
Swung through the vibrant music, till the air
Loaded with tinkling sounds and odors rare
Filters soul-deep within the fleshly mail,
Till, rapt, escaping from the body's jail,
The spirit issuing through its portal flies
To fairy realms of wonder and surmise—
That were indeed a taste of Paradise!

BUT with no thought of this the sordid spy
     Cast on the masterpiece his curious eye.
He was a merchant, trained in every guile
Of trade—to fawn, to browbeat, and to smile

Careful to hold in every scheme he tried
Of fraud or rapine law upon his side.
His talon fingers in their trembling clutch
Pulled back the shadowing curtain overmuch,
And Selim, of his presence made aware,
Looked up and met the stranger's cunning stare
And frowned to note the hard and vulture trace
Of avarice on the man's ill-omened face.
The other answered with a smile compressed:
"Has Allah, O Selim, made the time of rest
Too long, or has he given too short a day,
That thus you work the noontide hour away?"
But Selim threw his head back at the word,
For all distasteful was the voice he heard,
Like some proud courser that with action grand
Tosses aside a strange caressing hand,
And answered, " Little rest doth surely lie
With him, O merchant, who with prying eye
Looks either in the day-time or at night
On that which others fain would keep from sight,
Which none concerns.   To question not were best,
Whether I work at mid-day or I rest."

8

HE set aside the work of perfect art
    And waited for the stranger to depart,
Who turned his furtive, greedy glance upon
The perfume-holder ever and anon.
He named a price, but Selim shook his head;
That special thing was not for sale, he said.
The other, following his practised guile,
Answered again with unbelieving smile,
He had a friend named Marco, from the north,
Who, buying works of art, had ventured forth
From Venice even to the farthest East,
Would give the price of many a lordly feast
For such a thing as this, if he would sell:—
But Selim no persuasion might compel
To barter; wrathful that he still was pressed,
He locked his treasure in a cedar chest,
Then urged upon the merchant one by one
The less inspired works that he had done—
They were but few,—till forth the stranger went
And left him in his solitude content.

THE merchant paused when he was out of sight
    Of Selim's booth, his face with passion white;

9

With fingers clenched and with a frowning brow
He seemed to register some mental vow.
The swart Egyptian boy who stood before
A rich brass-dealer's widely swinging door,
Watched, with a keen and curious surmise
The knavish purpose in the stranger's eyes,
For every pantomimic act betrayed
Insatiate greed—the reckless lust of trade.

STRIDENT voice came calling from afar
The new-born hour—at once the clattering jar
Of hammers rose again upon the air;
The craftsmen hurried to the busy fair,
And through its alleys poured the human flood
Like buzzing bees a-swarm within a wood.
But Selim, in his resting hour intent
And keenly active, languid now was bent
Above his tinkering, as though toil had grown
Distasteful to him since the noon had flown.
His hammer strokes less eager, blow on blow,
Fell on the brass, grew slower and more slow,
And once he clasped his brow convulsive-wise,
As though it ached, and hid his downcast eyes.

IT was a hot and glaring afternoon;
   The hum in the bazaar like a bassoon
Grew constant—presently a shout of throngs
Came booming with the beat of drums and gongs,
While now and then the fitful snorting blast
Of trumpets on the echoing air was cast.
The shuffling sound of many slippered feet
Came like a wind-gust down the dusty street;
The loiterers left their seats beneath the walls,
Lured by the shouts and noisy trumpet calls;
The loud-tongued barter, with the hammering clashed,
Was stilled as by the glittering pageant flashed.
The last Shah's eldest son, 'twas bruited wide,
Was riding to the mosque to wed his bride,
Next to the Shah the first of Persian land
And named *The-Shadow-of-the-Sultan's-Hand;*
Yet, for his mother was of humble strain,
Who might not as an heir the throne attain.

BUT Selim, hooded in his changeless thought,
   Scarce heard the tattle which the gossips brought;
None sought to pass an easy word with him;
They deemed his silence but a surly whim.

He, heeding little what was thought or said
So that they left him quiet, in his head
Kept turning, like the burden of a swound,
One memory that coiled his mind around.
He let the lantern uncompleted stand
And from the little finger of his hand—
His left hand—with a pensive, wistful look,
He carefully a linen bandage took,
And this unwound, a tiny hammered thing
Of brass which bound his finger like a ring
Was shown, round which the tissue angry red,
Twinged fitfully as bit the figured shred.
He wet the cloth, replaced it; and a chime
Of thoughts went swinging backward to the time
When she, the idol of his heart, had stept
Across the doorway where his wares were kept,
And in a careless, blithely-mocking vein,
Had given him this little cirque of pain.
Ay, he remembered, how upon that morn
He felt with ecstasy his soul was born,
How he had gazed with flushed and rapt surprise
Upon her lissome form and laughing eyes,
Fairer than houri to the bosom pressed

Of Mahomet in the regions of the blest.
Except her eyes, which glittered each a star,
Her face was veiled, as in the white cymar
She glided through the market and by chance
Caught the obeisance and adoring glance
Of Selim, sitting cross-legged in his booth;
And as she saw the passion tide of youth
Sweep to his eyes, she smiled and oft again
Returned him salutation—now and then,
Paused for some moments at his little stall,
And then coquettishly, by letting fall
Some corner of her veil, like hide and seek,
Disclosed the rounded contour of her cheek
Of ripening olive, like the moon in mist,
And blush-rose lips that pouted to be kissea.

ONE day—'twas one of two such happy days
        As star perhaps a lifetime—through the ways
She came to visit Selim and to buy
Some trinkets of his patient industry.
Lingering she stayed an hour; made him tell
The way he wrought the brass; with playful spell
She drew from him the use of lead and pitch;

She took the die and punch and made him teach
Her hand to cut the ductile metal through;
One little die she held, 'twas virgin new—
A tiny whorl the pattern was—she tried
It on a strip of brass, and he, to hide
Her slender fingers from a missing blow,
Shielded them with his stouter hand, and so,
As once the stroke she missed, and still again,
He joyed to think for her he suffered pain.
At length she gave him back the die—he swore
With truthful look no one should use it more
Except himself, and he but on a gift
For her.   Her lustrous laughing eyes were lift
To Selim's face, as doubting, then with care
Mocking his earnestness, she told him where
An aged kinsman dwelt, whence he might take
The present he intended her to make.
Then into childlike playfulness did pass
Her mood; she took a tiny shred of brass,
And twisting it with pincers in a ring
Round Selim's finger tightly, tried to bring,
Mischievously, across the strong man's face
A wince, but failed, and smiling left the place.

AND Selim, never from that hour at rest,
    Had shrined her lovely image in his breast.
A few more times, as she had done before,
She to the market passed his open door;
But though his eyes with loving hunger sued,
That one sweet meeting never was renewed.
Now all his purpose to one issue ran:
Upon that day he straight for her began
The perfume-holder, lavished his fond heart
Upon it; for it eased him of his smart
To feel he wrought her service and to see
Its beauty growing like a stately tree,
Rooted in art, as with the tiny whorl
He would its richly shining round impearl
With wheels of light that glimmered on the view,
Fashioned to let the writhing pungent through.
For him she had one name and only one;
As with each noon the precious work was done,
He muttered as he placed with care apart
The gift, " 'tis for The-Star-of-Selim's-Heart."
The star that lighted up the lonely sky
Of his rapt spirit and then passed him by.

AND now 'twas finished—every tiny scroll
　　Was perfect—but the work in Selim's soul
Went ever onward like the incessant beat
Within his hearing, through the mid-day heat,
Of hammers in their tinkling changeless chime
Dinning industrious symphony to time.

HE took the punch-like tool, the slender die
　　That formed the whorl, and with a saddened eye
Defaced the pattern with his file and cast
The useless steel upon the street, then passed
His hand across his forehead as in pain,
And took the unfinished lantern up again.

BUT while he worked a warm Elysian dream
　　Fell o'er him like the sunset's dying gleam.
Upon the wings of passion forth he flew
To meet her where he'd held her oft to view
In fancy, all unknown to her; he thought
(Such strangeness in a dream is often wrought)
That she was now the seeker—he was—where?
He did not know, he did not seem to care—
But down the eddying current of his swound

There came some one and told him she had found
The perfume-holder—and then he straightway
Became the perfume-holder, and she lay
Caressing hand upon it and did speak
It fair and pressed it with her velvet cheek,
Letting her silk of hair, a shining pall,
Like Allah's blessing, o'er its richness fall.
Then for one moment, through the hammered brass
He felt his soul, the soul of Selim, pass
And thrill unto the magic of her touch;
The moment flitted—then came voices such
As Allah sends to true believers when
He tells them of the crooked ways of men,
That called, "O Selim! where is Selim?" soon
A voice made answer in a pleasant tune,
"I will find Selim, for I know him by
The ache within his finger;" then the sky
Was clouded with the sorrows, sighs, and pains
Of every soul that on the earth remains,
And forthwith went the form that held the voice
Among them, making from them all the choice
She knew was Selim's pain; with that began
By the dream process, building up a man

Like Selim, out of things that half-time fell
And crumbled in the falling; but the spell
Kept on till all was finished, head to feet;
Then, for one moment, Selim was complete,
Sitting in the bazaar, his right hand laid
Upon his hammer and the lantern stayed
Between his knees—but nowhere now was seen
The-Star-of-Selim's-Heart—naught but the sheen
Of brass-ware, and the crowd that thronged again
The market, talking of the marriage train.

'TWAS but a moment more—and the bazaar
Vanished again—upon an ivory car
He sat, the lovely lady by his side,
And she was wreathed with roses like a bride,
Starred all with jewels like the milky-way,
Or fair as dew-fall in the early ray
Of morning;—like the Shah's, his kaftan white
Blazed with a diamond, one deep fount of light
A Peri's tear-drop—and thus forth they rode
Midst cheers that wave on wave around them flowed,
Drawn by a gold and crimson harnessed span
Of cream-white horses, such as at Ispahan

The Shah drives slowly on great days of state,
Sitting in pomp of sovereignty sedate.
Flowers rained upon them, and their coursers' feet
Trod cloth of gold, as down the echoing street
They moved unto their bridal—till a band
With him, The-Shadow-of-the-Sultan's-Hand,
Met them, and a tumult thence arose—
For he, the prince, had claimed the bride—and blows
Were struck to blood . . . as Selim wounded lay,
His jewel and his bride were borne away.

AGAIN the vision changed—his memory fought
　　Against oblivion—he remembered what
Still made his finger ache—and she again
Was with him on a wild and lonesome plain.
A ponderous iron mace was in his hand;
Like mighty Rustem did he forward stand,
All husked in mail, and a tremendous boss
Of burnishd brass his aching arm across
Held up; a company of devils roared
Against him, and amidst the evil horde
Two Satans, fierce and hideous to view
As that White Demon god-like Rustem slew.

But the sweet lady far too much for fear
Loved him; she came his wounded hand anear
And kissed it, and the white Satans roared in scorn
Upon him, and his sinewy breast was torn
With passion, and he heaved his mace in air,
And rushing forward did for fight prepare.

WHEN suddenly he woke—his finger's pain
    Aroused him—he was in his stall again,
A poor brass-worker, his bright visions flown,
Unloved, ignoble, downcast, and alone.
A laughing crowd their jeers upon him kept,
For he had moved and muttered as he slept;
And foremost, as the laughter rippled long,
The crafty merchant stood amidst the throng.
He spake—"O Selim, your brave dreams must spin,
From poppy-head, or some old potent bin
Of wine of Shiraz! Those who hashish eat,
Go thus like fakirs through the crowded street
More strange adventures than were ever sung
By great Firdusi of the silver tongue."
And then continued, while the mirth ran high
And Selim gathered courage to reply—

'I too can dream, but not of ladies' lips
And battle, but of merchandise and ships;
For as in sleep I rested this mid-day,
I dreamed that Selim came and straight did say,
"'I have a perfume-holder here—'tis thine,
If thou wilt give me silver pieces nine;
Sell it to Marco, if thou seest fit
And let us both a profit make from it.'
I see my Selim sitting in his booth—
Say, has my vision spoken to me truth?"

"NO perfume-holder have I here for you,"
Said Selim, "all I sell is in your view."
The crafty merchant made him this repeat,
With guileful purpose, to the crowded street.
Still, once more he began—"But dreams are sent
From Allah "—"Some are, not yours"—Selim bent
His eye upon him, "I have these to sell;
If you have wish to purchase, it is well,
You shall have value straight and good; I need
Money to-morrow—make no further plead;
If of my wares you want not, forthwith cease,
And leave me, in the Name of Whom be Peace."

AT length the merchant bought of Selim's art
  With greed, yet loathing with his coin to part;
Then took his leave, and Selim, richer grown
By a few silver coins, could call his own
Nothing for sale, save where neglected lay
The unfinished lantern—now he worked away
Upon it fiercely, as though by this his thought
Might cease its whispering, or Time be brought
To mend his pace—and till the market gate
Was ready to be closed he lingered late
At work, when rising, with what anxious care
He fastened tight the little shutters where
The treasured gift, his pride and solace stood!
Then wandered forth in an unquiet mood.

THAT night, uneasy dreams without surcease
  Assailed his spirit, robbed him of his peace.
That one short night seemed fraught with danger more
Than all the hundred nights that went before
When he his treasure in the chest had kept
In the deserted market-place; he slept
But little, now that once he surely knew
Another lusted for it; on he threw

His clothes, and aimless wandered up and down
The winding streets and alleys of the town;
Still ever coming where his treasure lay
Behind the palisades which blocked the way
To the brass-workers' moonlit, still bazaar:—
The savage dogs, come baying from afar,
Leaped at the gate which held 'twixt them and him
As though they fain had torn him limb from limb.
A watchman with his lantern, on his round,
Drew near, attracted by the barking sound,
Looked at him, knew him, and passed otherwhere—
While he with steadfast eyes kept gazing there
Between the bars, toward where the shadow fell
Across his shop—a lonely sentinel.
Thus constantly until the dawn of day,
He lived the weary hours of night away.

SCARCE did the market barriers open drop,
     Than he again was hammering in his shop
At the unfinished lantern. He next took down
The perfume-holder; wrapped it, that the town
Might not view what he carried; then returned
All quickly home, and with the silver earned,

Adorned himself in splendid, rich array
As though it were for some high holiday;
Tied with deft care the perfume-holder too,
Within a silken cloth of creamy hue
In which he placed a scented billet, writ
In flowing verses when some rhyming fit
Had seized his spirit in the cool midnight—
A skilled caligrapher did it indite
With many a courteous phrase of love profound—
And all was with a flowery border bound.

LET me paint Selim's portrait, as he stands
     The perfume-holder lifted in his hands,
All garnished fair and ready for his part
Of service to the mistress of his heart.
The full fresh turban of white hand-wove stuff,
Embroidered with a glittering thread of buff,
A high topped hat of yellow camlet winds;
Beneath, a snow-white linen skull-cap binds
His temples with a narrow line, gleams fair
Above his bronzèd face and coal-black hair;
His head is straight, symmetric, small of size,
Alert as any steed's, and his dark eyes

Are lustrous like a steed's; an eager grace
Dwells in the outlines of his mobile face;
The lips are proudly set, the nostrils fine,
The features delicate and aquiline,
Surmounted by a wealth of crispy locks;
His tunic, brightened by the mazy flox,
Is like the turban white, and doth unfold
Now here or there the waving lines of gold;
A knife-case in the silken shawl is placed,
Which winds with graceful fold his slender waist
No statelier nor braver youth to see
From Shiraz to Khorassan is than he!

THE messenger he won to his emprise
    Was an old woman, good, discreet, and wise;
But ask me not the look, as he did place
His love-gift in her hands, of Selim's face,
Or while he watched her dragging steps depart
To her the one fixed Star-of-Selim's-Heart.
He lingered there, while soul and visage burned,
Waiting until the ancient dame returned.
Some hours later, back she came at last.
There was no need to question her, he cast

One look within her hands, where she did lift
Mutely toward his view the unopened gift,
Then said, " The lady, by the Shah's command,
Married The-Shadow-of-the-Sultan's-Hand."

THEN Selim bowed his head, and in that place
    A death-like pallor smote him in the face.
He tottered toward the door as though in years,
Pierced by a grief that struck too deep for tears.
Holding in numb embrace the brazen jar
He found himself again in the bazaar,
The while with quivering lips, distractedly,
He whispered texts of old philosophy,
Striving for consolation; but no heed
He gave them:—ah, how often in our need,
When earth is black beneath the blackened skies,
They fail, these peaceful sayings of the wise!

YET through his agony was woven a tune
    Of words that clogged his tongue and like a rune
Beat dull reiteration in his brain
And mingled with his bitter flow of pain:

" *WHETHER at Naishápúr or Babylon,*
Whether the Cup with sweet or bitter run,
The Wine of Life keeps oozing drop by drop,
The Leaves of Life keep falling one by one."

THESE were the words of one in Selim's town,
   Whose mighty spirit had brought high renown
To Persian land from every land abroad;
In Naishápúr they held him like a god;
He knew the amazing portents of the stars,
But yet his soul, foiled at life's prison bars,
Testing the hollowness of earthly state,
Mocked sadly at irrevocable fate,
And, spite of all he had by genius won,
Took up the olden tale of Solomon,
Chanting the dreary burden o'er again,
" 'Tis vain—the life we live, like death, is vain!"

AND Selim turned to work, because he felt
   His reason totter as he slowly spelt
The import of the blow upon his soul;—
In work, unceasing work, he might control
The sickness at his heart, and so, alas!

Might help the miserable days to pass.
He had forgot or had not cared to change
His holiday vestments; down the lengthened range
Of the bazaar the whole brass-working tribe
Broke forth upon him with loud laugh and gibe,
That bit not like the fangs of anguish grim,—
Yet like a swarm of gnats they worried him;
Longing to be alone, his soul felt wronged
As round his path the coarse mechanics thronged
With mock obeisance, gestures rude, uncouth,
Jeering, as they pursued him to his booth—
For little love they bore him.   Taunt him well!
Was he not Selim the Unsociable,
Too proud to mingle with his equals there?
They crowded close to see how he would stare
(For a surprise awaited him) as he,
Drunk with despair's unmanning ecstasy,
Unto his small store plodded heavily.

THE booth was plundered—all his wares were gone!
   And worse—his tools! he could not think upon
Their loss; their value was not great, but dear
Almost as were his fingers;—misery drear

Settled upon him; only now remained
The unfinished lantern, but deformed and stained,
As though the plunderer held its value light
And set his heel upon it out of spite.

HE sat a long time in his little shop
    Without a motion, with his head a-prop
Upon his hands, a ruined man, bereft
Of all he held most dear; to him was left,
When he a little cleared his mind to think,
And reason halted upon madness' brink,
Only the gift returned which he still held,
The perfume-holder; he will be compelled
To purchase bread and tools; now he will go
And from the merchant buy a lease of woe.

A BLURR and deafness fell on eye and ear—
    Confused him—nor his senses grew more clear
Till he before the merchant took his stand,
The precious piece of brass within his hand.
The place he looked upon with goods was rich;
Fine armor blazed from many a stand and niche;
Sabres from Samarcand and costly shawls

From Indian looms were hanging on the walls,
And Orient ivories, carvings from the Isles,
Within their lacquered cabinets stood in files.
The shelves were heaped with stuffs of rich brocade;
Mirrors of steel with silver frames inlaid
With jewels, glittering daggers, hookahs fine,
And all the costly wares of Levantine
And Indian markets, crowded all the space.
As Selim gazed with wonder round the place
Coarse faces covered him with leering scan,
Fit tools of service to the sordid man
Whose slaves they were, and downcast Selim felt
The transient courage he had groped for melt
Clean from his heart—his one despondent thought
Made desolation—all things 'gainst him wrought
A vast conspiracy—for the merchant now
Began with smiling and contemptuous brow
To scorn, to cheapen, and to vilify
That he had been so eager once to buy;
Then asking Selim what his need might be,
He told him he would take as surety
The handiwork and lend him; sadly then
Said Selim, " I need brass and tools again

To carry on my trade." The merchant's smile
Changed to a cold and stealthy look of guile
As forth he brought a well-assorted pack
Of half-worn tools; but Selim started back—
Then clutched—the things were his! faintness did seize
Upon him and he felt his spirit freeze
And shrivel; distant, indistinct, and small
Looked all things round him—darkness seemed to fall.
He was not sure he had been telling how
The tools were his, or still quite calmly now
That they were stolen from him, or that dumb
He had been standing, deathlike, dazed, and numb.
Suddenly came the merchant's hateful face
Close to his own, with horrible grimace;
Forth sprang two monstrous hands, that straightway lay
Grasp on his brazen treasure and away
Bore it in triumph to a distant shelf;
Then rushed the hot fit on; he flung himself
In rage against the servants—wildly fought—
Until his mind a little space was brought
To hear men's voices dwindling through the dim
From faces that he knew; one said of him
After another, Selim's could not be

The perfume-holder—they were sure that he
Owned nothing of the kind—they knew him well
And all his work—he yesterday did tell
He had not such a thing;—and as he strove,
Struggling, to right himself, they dragged and drove
Him forth, and nothing but a blurr was there
Of dust and pressure, anger and despair.
Blows rained upon him; one last cruel stroke
Felled him with torture;—then his spirit broke!

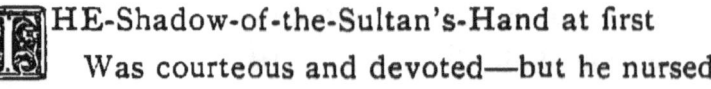

SHE, who had been to one unhappy heart
    The load-star of its being, sat apart
In the zenana's silken privacy,
A married captive, never to be free.
But o'er The-Shadow-of-the-Sultan's-Hand
Some time she ruled;—the heart she could command
Of that fierce fighter in his pleasant mood;—
A second wife, in sovereign solitude,
All gave her homage, all her triumph graced,
Even she, the first wed, whom she had displaced.

THE-Shadow-of-the-Sultan's-Hand at first
    Was courteous and devoted—but he nursed

Higher ambition than in flowers to bind
His spirit to the rule of one girl mind,
Howe'er enchanting, for his heart was set
On deeds of violence; he could ne'er forget
The zest for blood which followed him from birth;—
He was a bold, intrepid son of earth,
A graceful tiger in a leash of silk,
As mild and pleasant as the cocoa's milk,
When free from passion, but resolved and strong
And masterful when purpose swept along
His rapid tide of mind;—a lion hunt
In which he ever bore the danger brunt,
Or thought of some resistless, vengeful raid
Into Afghanistan, more often swayed
The councils of his heart, than any charms
He found within the circle of her arms.
And she, poor lonely discontented dove,
Brooded upon it, felt if she in love
Had been so favored in her lot to fall
Unto the heart that loved her all in all,
However lowly, howsoe'er distressed
By circumstance—by poverty oppressed—
Life had been happier, shared with such a one,

Than that now passed with this proud monarch's son.
Unlike the frivolous, tranquil, idle crew
Who chattered round about her, often grew
Intolerable to her vivacious mind
The still zenana—health and spirit pined.
But came distress far greater when, one day,
Returning from some distant wide foray
Into Afghanistan, her husband brought
A captive home, who now held all his thought.
The superseded wife grew languid, pale;
Till—part by some new thought to countervail
Her weak depression, part, she might consult.
A learned astrologer, whose art occult
In all that region was most famous—they
Who lived about her counselled her one day,
She should a few leagues' distant journey take
(The sad monotony of her life to break),
Apast the turquoise hills, and level land
That fringed the province with its shifting sand.

POOR lonely star of one lone heart! some love
    Her soul still yearned for like that heaven above
The Frankish women sought—she had not dreamed

That it had crossed her;—its pale radiance gleamed
Athwart her vision through her veil of tears,
Fairer as grew the distance of the years!
Bravely again she took life's burden up.
Hope flowered once more; she had not drained the cup
Of bitter vintage to its turbid lees.
She and her escort started as the breeze
Of early evening swept the scented glades
And waved the banners o'er long colonnades,
Ruffled the citron blooms, and filled the air
With cool perfume and freshness everywhere,
Rolled like cocoons the streamers of the sky,
Soothed the hot valleys with its fitful sigh,
Fluttered the folds of shawls and turbans loose
And frolicked in the billowy white burnous,
The heated city fanned with dewy breath,
And even revived the falt'ring pulse of death!

SERVANTS and slaves upon the camels laid
      The tents and baggage; others were arrayed
To take the journey, sitting on the packs
That hung to either side the camels' backs.
And as a guard, to rearward and before,

Some twenty warriors on their camels bore
Long lances, sceptres for each humpy throne,
Like staves of ancient kings in days unknown.

THE camel train from out the gateway passed
And left the hills behind—then travelled fast
Across the waste, whose open length was soon
O'erhung by the large lemon-colored moon.
The guards from time to time their challenge sent
To plodding footmen on their passage bent
Unto the city walls, who straightway told
Themselves as home-bound miners; they did hold
A moment (after they the mines had passed),
A band of all these travellers the last;
And, at the captain of the train's demand
Why they were journeying in that lonely land,
They answered humbly, they had carried out
Into the distant desert thereabout,
The corpse of one who had died raving mad
In prison; stripped the body what it had
Of worth upon it—now but from their toil,
With their poor recompense of sordid spoil.
The captain forward turned his camel's head
And told his lady what the men had said.

NAUGHT further marked their travel; all next day
They camped—at evening took again their way;
And when at last arose the second sun
They left the desert, their long journey done;
And to the village now their lady brought,
Where lived the famed astrologer she sought.

AFTER some messages had been exchanged,
A visit for the lady was arranged
To the astrologer:—his house was small
And undistinguished; but upon the wall
Of a rich room where he received his guest,
A time-piece hung of rarest art; impressed
With mystic figures stood an astrolabe
Fine wrought in brass when science was a babe,
Brought from Egyptian land; an open book
Lay on a table; in a crypt-like nook
Were yellow parchments piled. The languid wife
Wistfully eyed the man of learnèd life;
A sage sedate—a form of mark and note,
Where even a beggar in his frowsy coat
Looks almost like a king—his tall black cap
And simple flowing robe of woolen nap

Were of the finest, and his brow and eye,
Majestic, as through gazing on the sky
And pondering deeply o'er its hidden lore
He much of its sublime expression wore.
Full to the waist, wide o'er the massive chest,
His sable beard swept down his scarlet vest,
Lending grave dignity and benignant grace
Unto his lofty form and thoughtful face.
This saying rose from those who saw him then,
That "no men should wear beards but Persian men."

THE sad-faced lady, come to seek his aid,
    Took courage as his features she surveyed—
Calm, courteous, wise, he seemed; she told him all
Was needful for his science; told the thrall
And empty hunger of her heart, and, too,
Briefly her history, for she saw he knew
Much of the weakness of worn souls, for he
Was deeply read in the philosophy
And poetry of Iran and the East,
And soothed her hungry spirit with a feast
Of thoughtful phrases culled for counsel by
Men's souls to comfort life's extremity,

Down from the words of Solomon the Wise
To the star-gazer poet, he who lies
In her own city in unfevered rest,
The burial stones and clods across his breast.

THE words of counsel past, ere she her way
        Took thence, he told her, he the following day
The issue of his studies of the night
Would send her.   She too watched the twinkling light
Of stars, that maze-like through the heavens kept
Mysterious way:—beneath them mortals slept
As though no seeds of fate within them lay:—
Keepers of how many secrets they
Of human hearts, revealers of how few,
Though they eternal shine upon our view.
Ah, they did never to her soul impart
That one had called her "Star-of-Selim's-Heart!"

NEXT morn, in scented silk the missive came:
        TO the Most High and Honorable Dame,
        Wife of The-Shadow-of-the-Sultan's-Hand,
Fairest of all the fair of Persian land !
In name of Allah, whom the Faithful call
The Merciful, Victorious, Chief of All ;—

The Stars, O Lady, speak the truth, but man
Not always can their mystic answer scan ;
Such power seldom is to mortals given ;
I thrice to-night have read the face of heaven,
And thrice this answer hath been given to me—
                    "A FLIGHT OF BLACKBIRDS."
                              May it rest with thee,
O Lady, to interpret them aright,
And may they throw upon thy darkness light
According to thy heart ; and may the peace
Of Allah, who alone gives souls increase,
Be shown to thee.   This is the prayer devout
Of him the unworthiest of thy servants ; doubt
Not He will send thee grace.
                         Written by the hand
Of Hassan of the Astrolabe, to command.

SHE, taking these words with her, now began
      Her homeward journey, pondering; still ran
Her thoughts along one line; her mind was bent
Upon the answer of the stars; it went
Ever before her like a vision blest,
Guiding her to the hopeland of her quest.

IT was that chill and silent time of night
     Preceding sunrise, ere the dawning light
Grows creeping on the world; mysterious hour,
When Azreal comes with all his awful power
To loose the souls of men and women old
From out their bodies, and to close enfold
Their fluttering spirits—beareth them away
Unto the realms of midnight or of day.

THE camel-train paced slowly; rose the dust
     As each huge foot into the sand was thrust,
And fell again full quickly, beaten down
By the damp air; to right and left a frown
Against the sky betokened hills; the sun
Above the left ones soon his course to run
Prepared; the watchful guards from time to time
Turned in their saddles to behold him climb
The hill-tops; o'er the desert's darkened gray,
Ahead of them, the lighter film of day
Pressed a faint outline; an uneven spur
Dimly defined against the misty blur,
Breaking the outline showed them Naishápúr.

AS peered the sun's brow o'er the hills again,
Startled by that or by the camel-train,
A clamorous flight of birds upon one hand
Streamed from some object on the distant sand.
The lady, resting in uneasy sleep,
Awoke, as o'er her rose the rattling sweep
Of wings, and from her litter watched them float
Ominous and black against the heaven remote,
New lighted by the half-way risen sun,
Which o'er the pallid sky his splendor spun.
Back to her mind, as from a written page,
There rushed the words of the star-gazing sage,
"A flight of blackbirds "—then she waved her hand
And gave the captain of the train command
She must be taken straightway to the spot
Whence came the birds of omen—but he not
Without remonstrance did her will, soon day
Would scourge the desert with his burning ray.
As moved the slow procession toward the place
The sun gazed o'er the hill-tops—from his face
His streaming golden locks were shaken wide
And swept the landscape upon every side.

"**O** FAIREST lady," said the chief, in tones
          Sore vext, "let Allah hear me, 'tis the bones
But of a man, one lost or made away
With in the desert; others for a prey
Than these same birds have found him; there abides
With him no coin, nor weapons at his sides."
"In name of Allah, Merciful and Just,
Dismount, some of you men, and straightway thrust
Around him; search each bit of cloth and bone
To see if aught about him may be known."

U NWILLINGLY, and cursing the delay
          Unto themselves, they did her wish obey.
They lifted with their spears each ragged clout
And with their muskets moved the bones about.

"**N** OTHING, fair lady, nothing," said the chief,
          Climbing upon the saddle with relief;
Then set the rest in motion, well content
To quit their tarrying.   To the litter went
Some minutes after one who lingered late;
Without a word, but with a smile sedate,
Handed his lady in a tiny thing

Of white and yellow; round it was a ring
Or shred of brass, twist tight, that bore along
Each edge at intervals impression strong,
Irregular, a little whorl, which she
Looked at, surmising of its history,
Holding it in the hollow of her hand
Some moments, till her memory might expand
Around it, and revive the distant day
That she on Selim's finger in her play
Had twisted it, and limn the constant gaze
He ever held for her along the ways,
And all the tender love and rapt surprise
That lighted up his dark and thoughtful eyes.

TO this, then, he had come! Ay, well—alas!
    She knew the little pattern on the brass
As tearfully she scanned it—he had said
(She now remembered) in his little shed,
He, poor dead Selim, her lone worshipper,
The tool that made it, save on gift for her,
He ne'er would use; yes, he whose bones now lie
Scattered upon the sand, beneath the sky,
All except this one, this small finger-bone,

Pledge of his love which she possessed alone,
The one cold token of his constant flame,
Around which thoughtless beauty toiled to frame
A ring; on whose dry whiteness beauty now
Shed tears, pressed kisses, then with head a-bow
Laid it within her fair grief-laden breast
To cherish it and rock it there to rest.

THE lusty sun stared fiercely from on high
    When they attained the city.   The blue sky
Was dazzling clear, save where some fine-combed clouds
Straggled across it like the souls in shrouds
Speeding to heaven, or travellers single file
Moving one way, apart, suspecting guile,
Wrapping their parching bodies from the glare
And dusty highway.   The zenana's air
Unto the Star-of-Selim's-Heart was cool
And comforting, as fresh from out the pool
Of scented water on the rich divan
She lay and o'er her waved an Indian fan
Held by her favorite maid:—two little girls,
The pets of the zenana, bright as pearls,
Brought her a present which he did command,

Her lord, The-Shadow-of-the-Sultan's-Hand,
On her return be given her.   Carelessly
She loosed the first silk wrappings—paused—for she
Saw now it was a noble work of art,
Even such a love-work as some loyal heart
Like Selim's might have given her:—she unwound
The silk with wakened care, in thought profound;
A triumph of beauty! he had promised sure
Even such a gift;—alas! he had been poor.
Each thing within his little shop was rare,
But naught therein with such work could compare
As this great perfume-holder—for indeed,
Out of his poverty—from his daily need—
He had not time, perchance, with his employ,
But to begin for her some little toy.
Faint murmurings were thronging in her ears,
She gazed upon it through a mist of tears;
Seen midst them, the entrancing graceful thing
Seemed indistinct, gigantic, wavering.

A
S the tears fell she wiped them fast away;
        Then seeing more clearly, something made her lay
Grasp on the brazen vessel, while her gaze

Grew to it all excitement and amaze—
Then to her bosom pressed it with a sob:
As her heart, answering with a mighty throb,
Shook deep her being, all her shrine of hair
Closed round the perfume-holder like a prayer!

HERE—there—and there again the proof of love,
    Each scrolled and burnished strip of brass above,
Upon each ornamental fillet's round,
The same neat-patterned tiny whorl was found!
The same which on his finger once, amused,
She fastened—from the die herself had used!

YES, Selim's gift had come to her—his love
    Had found her after death—and there above,
Even in the far realms of bliss, new cheer
Must come to him; had she not grown more near
Unto his spirit though his outcast bones
Lay bleaching on the desert's sands and stones,
All save this finger-token?   But there—look!
Carved on the brass, his words—the open book
Of Selim's love—the words he never said
In life—his message to her from the dead!

HE sun that evening, from the spot the train
    Had halted when the day broke o'er the plain,
Might then be seen soft barred with roseate streaks
Dying away between the western peaks;
And as he sank from view, the cooling breeze
Of evening rustled in the breathing trees,
But rose at night, and with persistent sweep
A requiem along the wastes did keep,
And as it wailed its dreary, weird refrain
Around the hills and o'er the barren plain,
Cast heavy handfuls of soft sand where lay
A dead man's bones—and when the face of day
Looked for them, lo! the desert held its trust,
Folded forever in its shroud of dust!

ON that same night, the wind with plaintive sigh
    Entered a lonely cloistered turret high
Of the zenana of a prince, and there
Searched out a dim-lit chamber, lifted rare
Spiced odors forth along the midnight air
From a brass perfume-holder—such sweet breath
As rises only at a monarch's death.

48

I N the starred duskness, pale and dreamy-eyed,
     A woman breathed the incense—watched it glide
Out toward the desert; one hand on her breast,
Dove-like against the quivering whiteness, pressed
A silken case—within, a little bone
And piece of hammered brass. . . .
                              No more is known.

49

www.ingramcontent.com/pod-product-compliance
Lightning Source LLC
Chambersburg PA
CBHW030901260626
47169CB00008B/2632